HOW TO DRAW
PETS

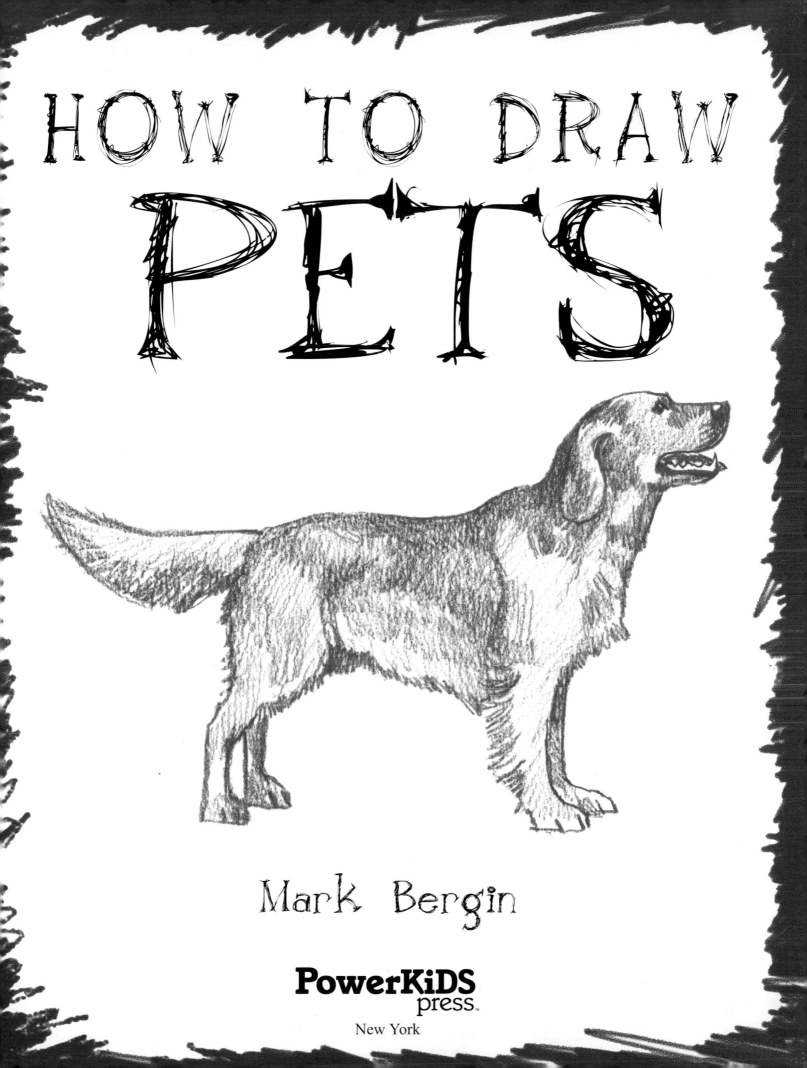

Mark Bergin

PowerKiDS
press™

New York

Published in 2012 by The Rosen Publishing Group, Inc.
29 East 21st Street, New York, NY 10010

Editor: Rob Walker
U.S. Editor: Kara Murray

Library of Congress Cataloging-in-Publication Data

Bergin, Mark.
How to draw pets / by Mark Bergin. — 1st ed.
    p. cm. — (How to draw)
 Includes index.
  ISBN 978-1-4488-4511-8 (library binding) —
 ISBN 978-1-4488-4517-0 (pbk.) —
 ISBN 978-1-4488-4523-1 (6-pack)
 1. Animals in art—Juvenile literature.
 2. Drawing—Technique—Juvenile literature. I. Title.
  NC783.8.P48B47 2012
  743.6—dc22

                                                2010049184

Manufactured in China

CPSIA Compliance Information: Batch #SS1102PK: For Further Information contact
Rosen Publishing, New York, New York at 1-800-237-9932

PAPER FROM
SUSTAINABLE
FORESTS

Contents

Making a Start

Learning to draw is about looking and seeing. Keep practicing and get to know your subject. Use a sketchbook to make quick drawings. Start by doodling and experiment with shapes and patterns. There are many ways to draw. This book shows only some methods. Visit art galleries, look at artists' drawings, see how friends draw, but above all, find your own way.

Make a range of sketches, from more detailed to quicker sketches, to trying to capture the form of the animal as quickly and accurately as possible.

Make a note of any of your subjects' features that may help later when doing a complete drawing, such as its coloring and any outstanding features.

Drawing Materials

Try using different types of drawing paper and materials. Experiment with charcoal, wax crayons, and pastels. All pens, from felt-tips to ballpoints, will make interesting marks. You could also try drawing with pen and ink on wet paper.

Felt-tip

Silhouette is a style of drawing that uses only a solid black shape.

Ink

Lines drawn in **Ink** cannot be erased, so keep your ink drawings sketchy and less rigid. Do not worry about mistakes as these lines can be lost in the drawing as it develops.

Hard **pencils** are grayer and soft pencils are blacker. Pencils are graded from #1 (the softest) to #4 (the hardest).

Charcoal is very soft and can be used for big, bold drawings. Ask an adult to spray your charcoal drawings with fixative to prevent smudging.

Pastels are even softer than charcoal, and come in a wide range of colors. Ask an adult to spray your pastel drawing with fixative to prevent it from smudging.

Perspective

If you look at any object from different viewpoints, you will see that the part that is closest to you looks larger, and the part farthest away from you looks smaller. Drawing in perspective is a way of creating a feeling of depth, or of showing three dimensions on a flat surface.

The vanishing point (V.P.) is the place in a perspective drawing where parallel lines appear to meet. The position of the vanishing point depends on the viewer's eye level. Sometimes a low viewpoint can give your drawing added drama.

V.P.

V.P.

V.P.   V.P.

Two—point perspective uses two
vanishing points. There is one for lines
running along the length of the subject,
and one on the opposite side for lines
running across the width of the subject.

Three—point perspective uses
a third vanishing point for lines
running vertically, or up or
down. This gives a very realistic
three—dimensional effect.

V.P.   V.P.

High eye level
(view from above)

V.P.

V.P. = vanishing point

Heads, Paws, and Claws

Pets have many different types of heads, paws, and claws. Studying and sketching the detailed features of a pet will help you with your final drawings.

Quick pencil sketches can help you understand the structure of paws and claws.

Look for areas where tone should be darker and also for changes in texture.

The more you study a subject and practice drawing it, the more accurate your drawings will become.

Try to capture as much detail
as you can in your sketches.

Look carefully at the size and
shape of the eyes, ears, and nose.
Note the length of the whiskers.

Always consider the light source and
add tone to the darker areas.

Using Photos

Drawing from photographs of pets can help you develop both your drawing skills and your eye for detail.

Make a tracing of a photograph and draw a grid of squares on it.

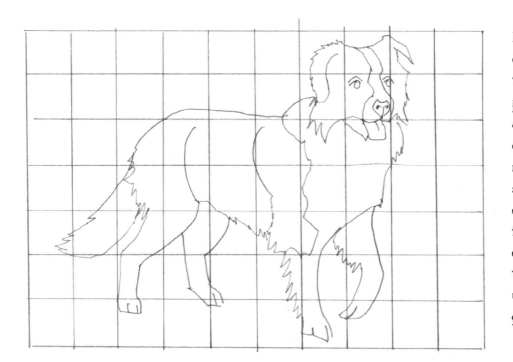

Now take a piece of drawing paper of the same proportions and draw another grid on it, either enlarging or reducing the square's size. You can now copy the shapes from each square of the tracing to the drawing paper, using the grid to guide you.

Light source

Light source

To make your drawing look three—dimensional, decide which side the light source is coming from, and put in areas of shadow where the light does not reach.

Sketch in an overall tone and add surrounding textures to create interest and a sense of movement. Pay attention to the position of your drawing on the paper. This is called composition.

Cat

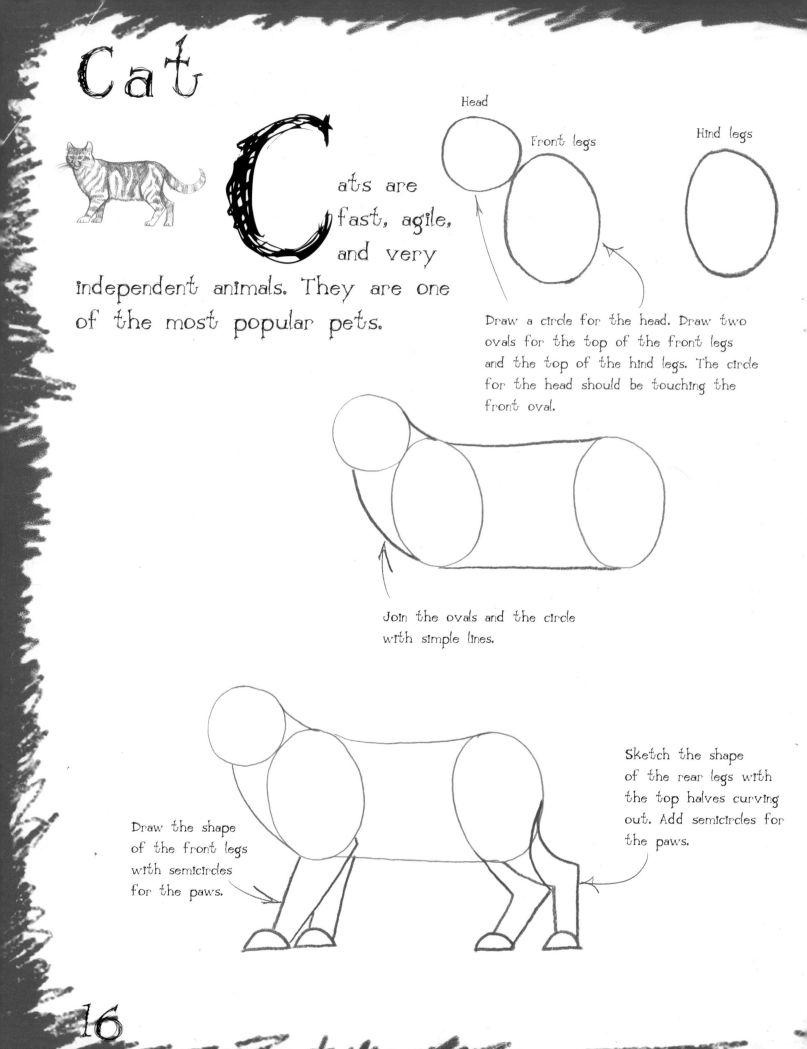

Cats are fast, agile, and very independent animals. They are one of the most popular pets.

Head

Front legs

Hind legs

Draw a circle for the head. Draw two ovals for the top of the front legs and the top of the hind legs. The circle for the head should be touching the front oval.

Join the ovals and the circle with simple lines.

Draw the shape of the front legs with semicircles for the paws.

Sketch the shape of the rear legs with the top halves curving out. Add semicircles for the paws.

Position triangular shapes on top of the head for ears, circles for eyes, and basic shapes for the mouth and nose.

Add two long lines for the tail.

Add lines to define the paws.

Complete the head details. Add short hair inside each ear and whiskers on each side of the face.

Shade in the cat's eyes and leave a lighter area around them to help them stand out.

A series of short lines gives the cat striped fur.

Add jagged lines around some edges of the cat's body to create fur.

Remove any unwanted construction lines with an eraser.

Hamster

Small, furry hamsters have large cheek pouches for carrying food.

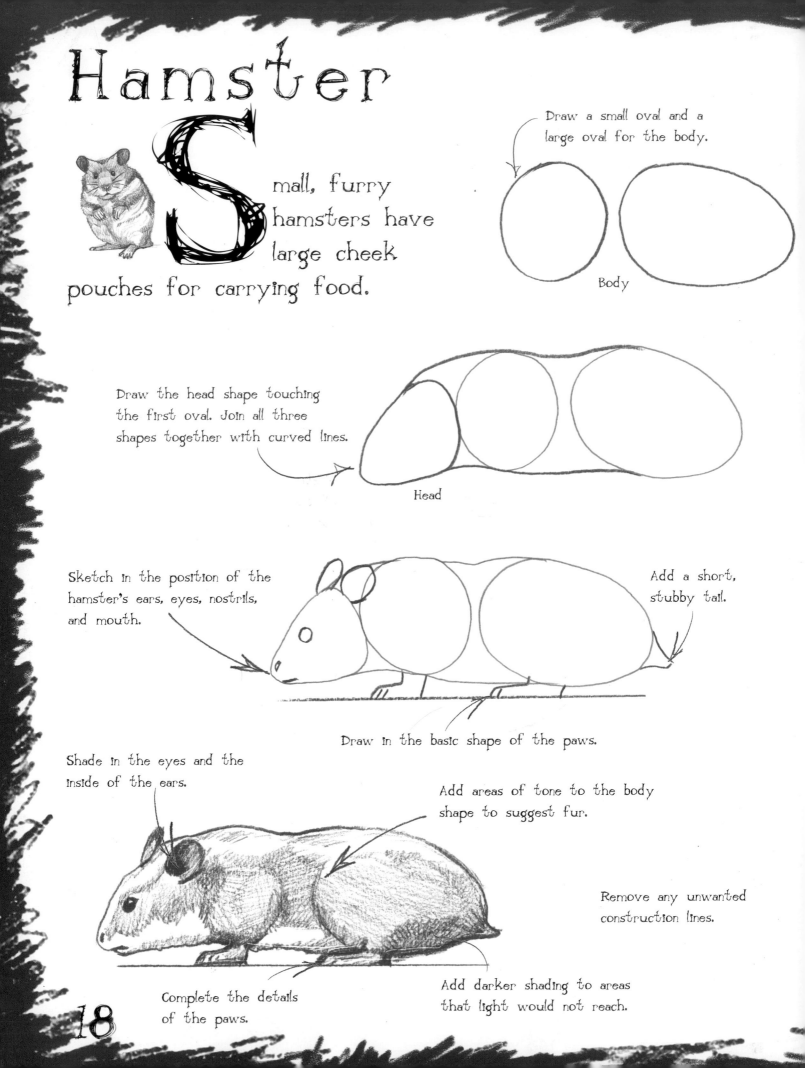

Draw a small oval and a large oval for the body.

Body

Draw the head shape touching the first oval. Join all three shapes together with curved lines.

Head

Sketch in the position of the hamster's ears, eyes, nostrils, and mouth.

Add a short, stubby tail.

Draw in the basic shape of the paws.

Shade in the eyes and the inside of the ears.

Add areas of tone to the body shape to suggest fur.

Remove any unwanted construction lines.

Complete the details of the paws.

Add darker shading to areas that light would not reach.

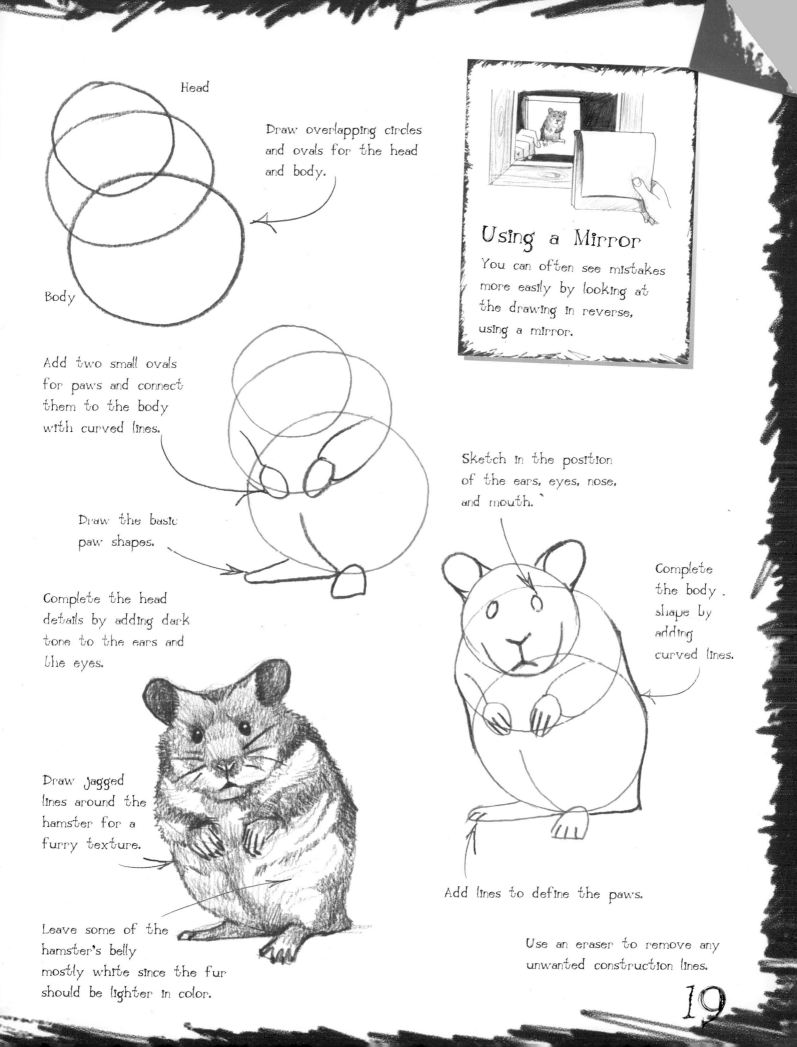

Head

Draw overlapping circles and ovals for the head and body.

Body

Using a Mirror

You can often see mistakes more easily by looking at the drawing in reverse, using a mirror.

Add two small ovals for paws and connect them to the body with curved lines.

Sketch in the position of the ears, eyes, nose, and mouth.

Draw the basic paw shapes.

Complete the body shape by adding curved lines.

Complete the head details by adding dark tone to the ears and the eyes.

Draw jagged lines around the hamster for a furry texture.

Add lines to define the paws.

Leave some of the hamster's belly mostly white since the fur should be lighter in color.

Use an eraser to remove any unwanted construction lines.

19

Rabbit

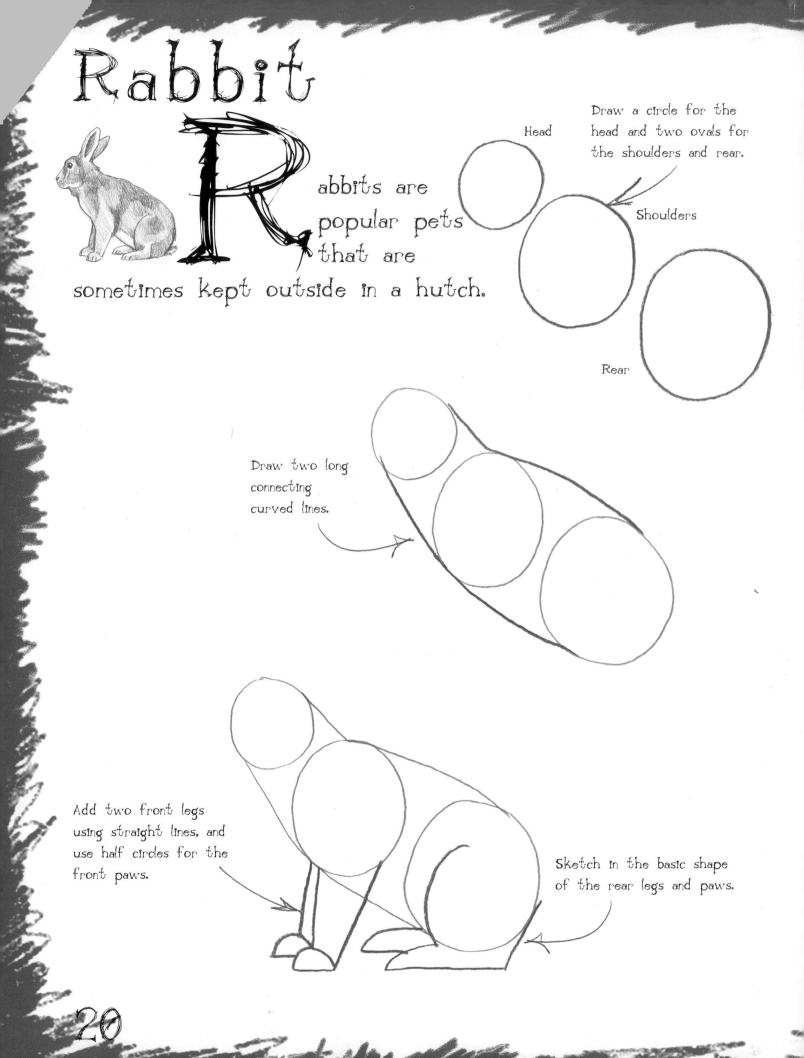

R abbits are popular pets that are sometimes kept outside in a hutch.

Draw a circle for the head and two ovals for the shoulders and rear.

Head

Shoulders

Rear

Draw two long connecting curved lines.

Add two front legs using straight lines, and use half circles for the front paws.

Sketch in the basic shape of the rear legs and paws.

Composition

By framing your drawing with a square or a rectangle, you can make it look completely different.

Position the rabbit's ears on its head.

Sketch in the rabbit's muzzle using straight lines.

Add a little round tail.

This drawing of a rabbit from a different angle shows all the construction lines used.

Add the head details. Draw in the ears, eyes, small nose, and mouth.

Add tone to the rabbit's body to give the impression of fur.

Add shading to areas where the light would not reach.

Remove any unwanted construction lines using an eraser.

21

Fish

Pet fish, with their bright colors, can be beautiful to look at.

Draw a long oval shape for the body of the fish and a small oval for its tail.

Body

Tail

Add a series of curved lines for the fins.

Add a small circle for the eye and put a dot in the middle.

Draw in curved lines to show the pattern on the fish's body.

Add tone to define the pattern and to create darker areas of shading.

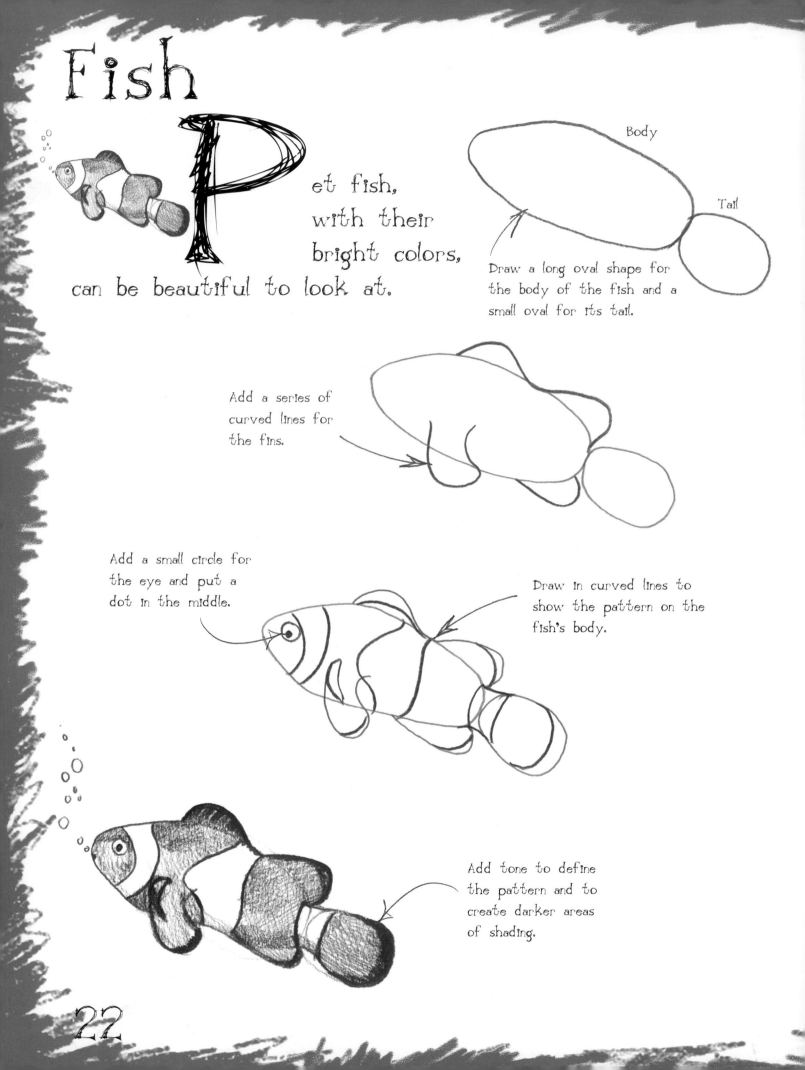

Fish fins are usually drawn as fine lines coming out from the body.

Many different types of fish can be drawn using the same basic construction lines for the body and tail fin. These can then be adapted to show different features.

The shape of the extra fins can be added depending on the type of fish you want to draw.

Add bubbles to create interest.

Drawing a center line shows which direction the fish is facing.

Using an eraser, remove any unwanted construction lines when the drawing is finished.

Parrot

Parrots are large, colorful birds that can often mimic a person's speech.

Draw two ovals for the parrot's head and body.

Head

Body

Join the head to the body with two curved lines.

Draw in the shape of the tail with two long lines.

Sketch in a simple tube shape as a perch.

Sketch in long curved lines to add the wing shape.

Draw the basic shape of the claws around the perch.

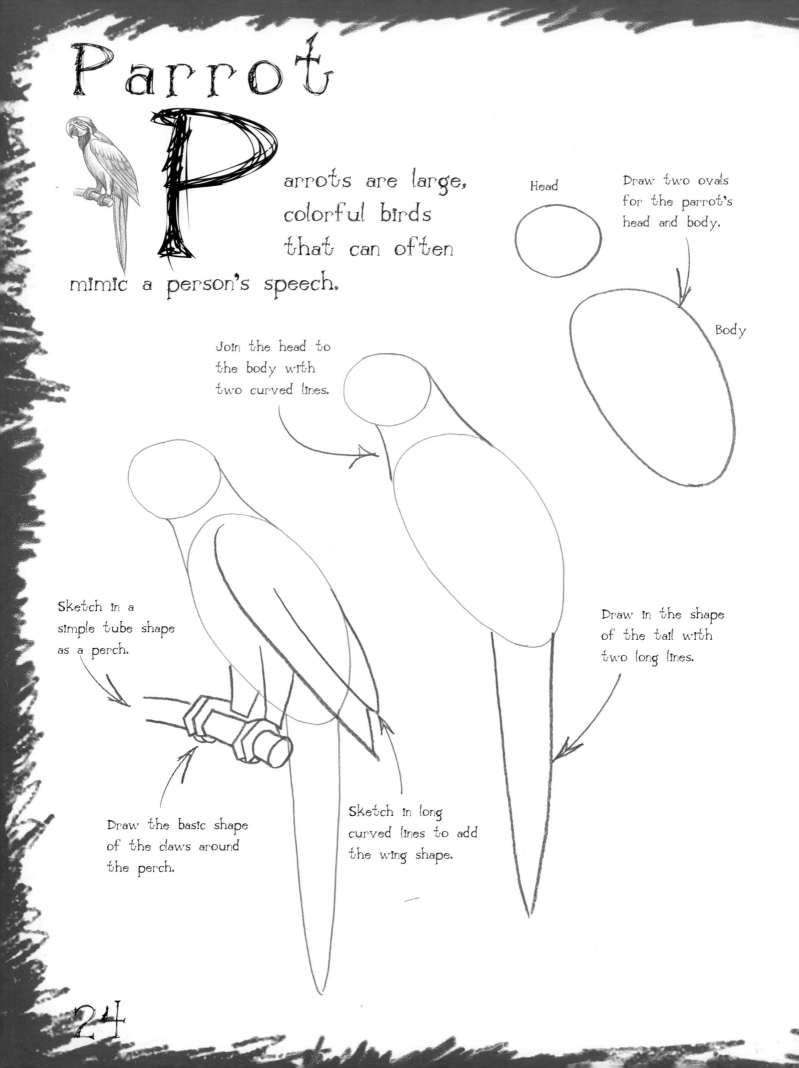

Add the eye and define the markings of the face and head.

Add in layers of feathers with a series of short, curved lines.

Draw in the hook-shaped beak.

Add tone. Leave the front of the beak white to create a reflective shine.

Carefully add the feather details to the face.

Divide the tail in two with one long line.

Add an area of dark tone under the head.

Parrot Parts

Study different parts of the parrot. Observe how its beak shape works or how individual feathers come together.

Add lines around the claws.

Add tone to define each of the feathers.

Use an eraser to remove any unwanted construction lines.

25

Mouse

Mice are small members of the rodent family and make good pets.

Draw three ovals, one for the head and two for the body. Connect the body shapes with a curved line.

Add in the basic shape of the front and back limbs.

Draw the eye shape.

Sketch in rounded shapes for the ears.

Sketch in paws at the end of each limb.

Draw two long, curving lines for the tail.

Add dark areas inside the ears.

Add patches of tone to create a fur texture. Pay attention to the direction of the tone to make it as realistic as possible.

Add whiskers.

Add detail to the tail.

These three examples show how to use the construction lines to draw a mouse in different positions.

Mice are very flexible. The body can look long or short depending on the angle from which you view it.

Fur can have many patterns and shades, so use different depths of tone to show these patterns.

Remove any unwanted construction lines using an eraser.

27

Snake

Snakes frighten many
people, but to others
they make great pets.

Draw one long,
curvy line for the
snake's spine.

Add an oval for
the head.

On either side of the
spine draw another two
long lines, which taper
together at the tail end,
for the body.

Add in the shape of the snake's head (see instructions below).

Add tone to the snake's body to give it a pattern.

Complete the head details, adding its eyes, nostrils, and tongue.

Add shadow under the snake depending on the direction of the light source.

A snake's head has a special shape. Create a construction line box as shown here to help you draw the head and features.

A drawing of a snake's head from the side shows the raised areas and position of the features.

Use an eraser to remove any unwanted construction lines.

29

Bearded Dragon

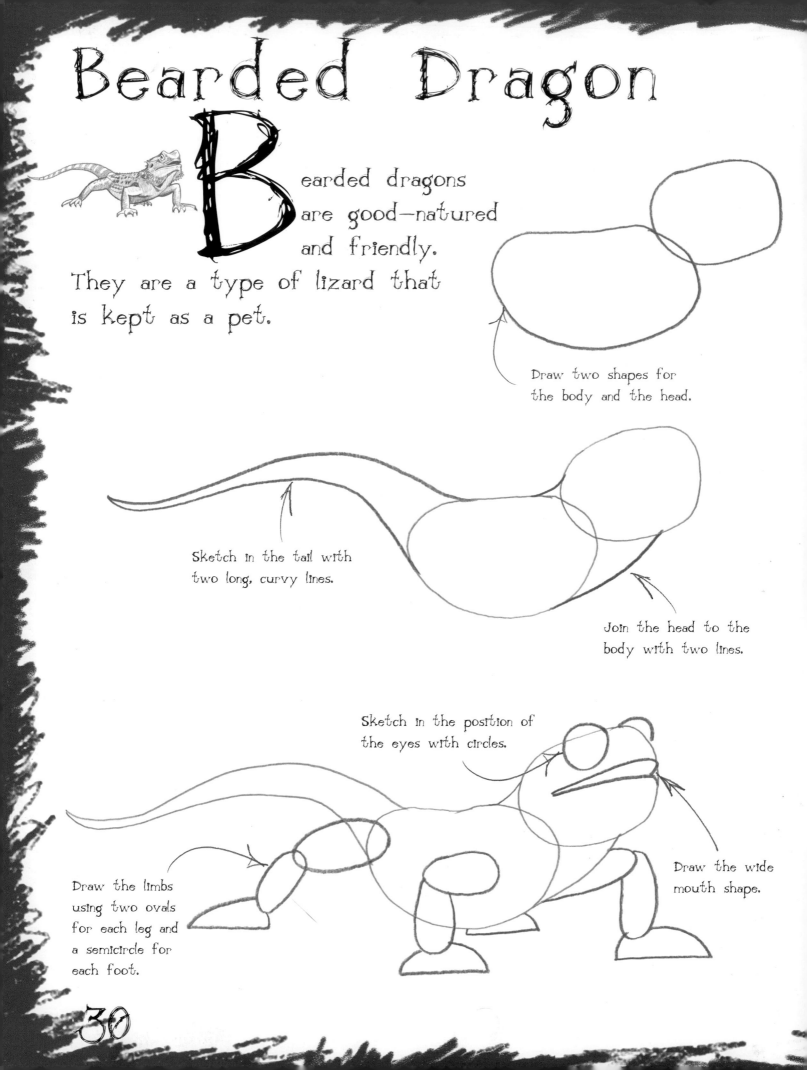

Bearded dragons are good-natured and friendly. They are a type of lizard that is kept as a pet.

Draw two shapes for the body and the head.

Sketch in the tail with two long, curvy lines.

Join the head to the body with two lines.

Sketch in the position of the eyes with circles.

Draw the wide mouth shape.

Draw the limbs using two ovals for each leg and a semicircle for each foot.

Draw the eye in the center of the circle.

Sketch jagged lines down the back and on the side.

Draw the claws on each foot.

Draw jagged lines to show the spikes fanning out from the back of the head.

Add a curved line to show the underside of the chin.

Add stripes to the tail using tone.

Add more ridges to the back.

Leave a highlighted area on top of the head to suggest its shiny scales.

Complete the sharp claws.

Add shading to any areas where light will not reach.

Complete the head details. Add an ear hole at the side of the head. Darken the inside of the mouth using tone.

Remove any unwanted construction lines with an eraser.

Glossary

composition (kom–puh–ZIH–shun) The arrangement of the parts of a picture on the drawing paper.

construction lines (kun–STRUK–shun LYNZ) Guidelines used in the early stages of a drawing. They are usually erased later.

fixative (FIK–suh–tiv) A type of resin that is sprayed over a finished drawing to prevent smudging. It should be used only by an adult.

galleries (GA–luh–reez) Rooms or buildings that show works of art.

light source (LYT SORS) The direction from which the light seems to come in a drawing.

perspective (per–SPEK–tiv) A method of drawing in which near objects are shown larger than faraway objects to give an impression of depth.

silhouette (sih–luh–WET) A drawing that shows only a flat dark shape, like a shadow.

sketchbook (SKECH–buhk) A book in which quick drawings are made.

texture (TEKS–chur) How something feels when you touch it.

vanishing point (VA–nish–ing POYNT) The place in a perspective drawing where parallel lines appear to meet.

Index

Web Sites

Due to the changing nature of Internet links, PowerKids Press has developed an online list of Web sites related to the subject of this book. This site is updated regularly. Please use this link to access the list:
www.powerkidslinks.com/htd/pets/